DIVORCE
AND YOUR FAMILY™

DIVORCE AND YOUR FEELINGS

VIOLA JONES AND RACHEL AYDT

ROSEN
PUBLISHING®

New York

Published in 2017 by The Rosen Publishing Group, Inc.
29 East 21st Street, New York, NY 10010

Library of Congress Cataloging-in-Publication Data

Names: Jones, Viola, author. | Aydt, Rachel, author.
Title: Divorce and your feelings / Viola Jones and Rachel Aydt.
Description: First Edition. | New York : Rosen Publishing, 2017. | Series:
  Divorce and your family | Audience: Grades 7-12. | Includes
  bibliographical references and index.
Identifiers: LCCN 2015043498 | ISBN 9781508171287 (library bound)
Subjects: LCSH: Children of divorced parents--Juvenile literature. |
  Emotions--Juvenile literature.
Classification: LCC HQ777.5 .J646 2017 | DDC 306.89--dc23
LC record available at http://lccn.loc.gov/2015043498

Manufactured in China

CONTENTS

INTRODUCTION

Have your parents recently had "the talk" with you? Not the one about the birds and bees, but the conversation in which they drop the bomb that they're splitting up? Maybe you saw it coming because your parents constantly argued and your house felt like a battleground. Or maybe it caught you completely off guard: sure, Mom and Dad don't spend much time together anymore, but at least they never fight. Either way, the announcement that your parents will no longer be married to each other will change your life forever, in ways that you can't even imagine yet.

Divorce in the United States is a common occurrence—around 45 percent of marriages end in divorce—so you are definitely not alone. There was a time not so long ago when divorce was considered scandalous and children of divorced parents lived with the shame of coming from a "broken home." Nowadays, for better or for worse, you are unlikely to be the only kid in your class whose parents aren't together.

This doesn't mean that divorce is easy to deal with. In fact, because it has become so prevalent in our society, many people

When you learn that your parents will be divorcing, you might not know how to cope with your feelings. You might get the sense that your life is over. While your family will change forever, it won't be as bad as you think.

underestimate the toll it takes on children, whether they are young kids or older teens. When your parents part ways, it can feel like your world is shattering. And in truth, life as you knew it is ending.

You will be going through lots of changes: maybe adjusting to a new home, new school, or even a new family. You might need to pitch in a lot more around the house, get a part-time job, or even appear in family court.

At the same time, you may be totally confused about your place in the family and how you're supposed to feel. And you might think you have no one to turn to. It is very easy during this time for parents to be focused only on their own problems, and you may have a hard time telling them how you feel. You may not be comfortable confiding in your friends or your favorite teacher. As a result, you can end up feeling confused and totally alone.

So, how can you cope with your feelings right now? It's hard enough to handle what comes up in life when everything is normal. How will you find the extra energy you'll need to console your parents? Or your siblings? What about yourself? How will you deal with moving back and forth between two households? Why do you feel responsible for having to make everything better? Why do you feel responsible for everything falling apart to begin with? What happens when you can't deal with your stepparents or stepsiblings?

Whatever your situation is, this resource will offer some advice on how to maneuver your way through this difficult time. Believe it or not, all of the feelings you're experiencing are normal. It may surprise you to learn that you have more power over your emotions than you might think. And even though you may feel alone, you aren't! In this resource, you'll find out how to find people who will support you.

Your opinions and emotions about your parents' divorce are important. By learning how to express them, confide in others about them, and work them out, the experience of divorce may not be all bad. Instead, it can be an incredible time of growth and independence for you.

Read on to learn what sounds impossible: how you can adapt the painful experience of divorce into one that helps you become a stronger person.

CHAPTER ONE

MY PARENTS FIGHT ALL THE TIME

When we think about troubled marriages, most of us think of parents fighting. Sometimes arguing can be healthy, and many relationships can benefit from it. But when fighting doesn't resolve issues and feelings are continuously hurt, it can be a sign of trouble.

Furthermore, parents whose relationship is in trouble don't necessarily fight at all. They may ignore each other altogether. Whatever form it takes, an unhappy parental relationship adds up to a lot of tension at home. You probably feel it yourself—how could you not?—but you may not know what it is or what to do with it.

I knew something was up when my parents started fighting like cats and dogs. And it was over such stupid stuff. My mom would yell at my dad for not doing anything around the house. When she wasn't nagging him, she would make snide comments about him under her breath. He'd get upset and scream that nothing he did was right. I tried to leave the room when they were fighting, but I could still hear them from my bedroom. — Bobby

It is upsetting when parents fight. They are two people who are supposed to love each other, but why does it sound like they hate each other? Fighting can be a healthy form of communication or a sign of bigger problems.

Bobby's situation is pretty common. It's not always easy to understand why parents fight. After all, it makes them feel terrible afterwards. But what's even worse is how it can make you feel—and you're not even the one in the fight! So what are you supposed to do when things get loud, angry, and scary at home?

Chances are, a lot of smaller struggles between your parents have been brewing for a while, and fighting is just the way the pent-up anger shows itself. It won't last forever, and it's important during this time to try to be as clear about your own feelings as possible—not just to your parents, but to yourself.

Put the Fighting in Perspective

It is difficult to figure out why your parents are at each other's throats all the time. Although the conflicts between your parents may run deep, tempers will often flare up over little things. Isolating a few of the sources of your parents' fights might make them seem smaller and more manageable to you.

Writing in a journal can help you find patterns in your parents' arguments. It also can help you identify your feelings about these fights. This activity might enable you to put things in perspective.

Remember that old phrase, "You're making a mountain out of a molehill?" Looking at each of the molehills individually can give you some perspective. Instead of saying, "My parents are in another huge and nasty fight," you can say to yourself, "Who cares that Dad dropped the plate? Big deal." Although you can't change the fact that they're not getting along, you can help put things in perspective.

FAMILY STRESS

There are some common problems in families that cause a lot of stress and may even lead to divorce. Perhaps there are too many bills to pay, and money's getting tight. Another common problem in families is alcoholism and drug abuse. If one of your parents has a problem, you are not alone. There are groups, such as Al-Anon, that you could get involved with that would help you out a lot if your parents suffer from alcohol or drug problems. These group meetings are confidential and can help you by introducing you to other people who are going through the same thing.

If there is any physical abuse going on in your house, you need to ask for help. One good person to speak with is your school counselor, who is trained to treat your problems with confidentiality and who can tell you whom to contact in your community.

The Dreaded Talk

Even the most thoughtful and caring parents can't put a good spin on divorce. It's a dreaded conversation when your parents sit you down and tell you they're splitting up.

One Sunday morning, my mom and dad sat down with me and my sister because they said they had something important to tell us. They were both really serious, and I got scared. My mom started by saying, "First of all, Daddy and

I want you to know that we love you both very much." Then Dad said, "Your mom and I have decided that even though we still love each other, we can't live together anymore. We're getting a divorce." — Jasmine

While her sister started to cry, Jasmine's stomach felt twisted, and her heart felt like it had jumped into her throat. At first she felt stunned, and then she felt sad. These feelings were also mixed in with fear, confusion, and uncertainty. She became increasingly nervous about how things were going to be in the future for her and her little sister.

No one wants to have "the Talk" with his or her parents. It's a moment when your life will change forever. It may be a long road ahead, but you'll be going through it together.

When your parents first tell you that they're getting divorced, it feels like your world is caving in around you. There is no doubt that this is going be a challenging and difficult time, but with a little guidance and thought, you can make it better. There are people you can talk to, groups you can join, books you can read, and many online resources you can go to for help.

Just about everybody has a friend whose parents have divorced. Maybe the friend was so young that he or she doesn't even remember going through it. Maybe your friend spends summers somewhere exotic with the other parent. Maybe he or she does not see the other parent at all.

No matter how a friend's situation turned out, remember that your situation is unique. Just because one friend's father moved away and she doesn't see him anymore does not mean that the same thing is going to happen to your family. Keep your cool and remember that for a little while, there will be some changes. You can get through it if you give yourself a break and take things one step at a time.

CHAPTER TWO

WHERE YOU STAND IN THE DIVORCE

Divorce sounds like a dirty word. It conjures up images of angry fighting, whispering neighbors, and confused children. If you are aware of these common associations with divorce, it's no wonder you're not sure how to feel about it.

After the initial shock of learning that your parents are splitting up, there will be a transition period. You might feel like your parents are ignoring you. Or you might find that they worry about you too much. But after your parents have dropped the bomb on you, what are you supposed to do? Go about your life like nothing has happened? And how are you supposed to feel? Is it ok to feel more than one thing?

Your Evolving Feelings

The truth is, your feelings might change from week to week, even day to day. You might be angry one day when your mom and dad cross signals and no one picks you up from practice. You might feel sad when you see your mom crying. And you might

Your parent might be overprotective during the transition that happens with divorce. He or she might worry about you more than usual. You might also have trouble adjusting to staying at each parent's house.

be confused when suddenly you and your siblings stay at your dad's new apartment every other weekend.

So how do you go from feeling confused, angry, ashamed, and sad to the positive things that can come as a result of divorce, like change, relief, expansion, learning, growth, and strength? One thing to know up front is that it may be a long road. You might not be able to recognize the positive aspects of your parents' divorce for months or even for several years.

It's Not Your Fault

One of the most important—but also most difficult—things to remember is that your parents aren't leaving you. They are splitting up as a couple because they couldn't make their marriage work. They aren't divorcing because of anything you did wrong. Parents have a whole host of issues that you aren't involved in. Their reasons for divorcing are most likely very complicated and might not mean much to you.

Still, it's easy to blame yourself for your parents' divorce. Take their fighting, for example. You might feel as if your parents are fighting because of you—something you did (or didn't do) or even the fact that you're there. Keep in mind that even if you do come up in their arguments, it's not your fault that they can't get along. Your parents love you no matter what they are fighting about.

Often adults argue over smaller things that suddenly build up. Or they may have been trying to work their problems out together privately for a long time, but ultimately they aren't able to reconcile. They may feel bitter or feel as if they failed. Whatever the reason, when things are tense, sometimes the smallest incident will set off an explosion.

Whose Side Am I On?

Even though you aren't getting a divorce, it doesn't mean that you're not affected by your parents' split. You are a member of the family and the household, and you will certainly have an opinion about what's being hashed out. Chances are, that opinion will sway in favor of one parent. Empathizing with one parent is normal right now, and you shouldn't feel guilty for doing so. This doesn't mean that you don't love your other parent; you might just be on the same wavelength as your mom or your dad right now.

The best way to stay out of the conflict of your parents' divorce is to steer clear of them. You might find that when your mom isn't

It's easy to feel like you are to blame when your parents argue. Maybe you've even been the subject of one of their fights. But be assured that you are not the reason they are divorcing.

around, your dad starts bad-mouthing her to you, or vice versa. It might feel good for that parent to blow off some more steam, but if you can't stand hearing it anymore, tell your parent that you don't want to be in the middle. If he or she gets mad at you, just remember that it is temporary. Your parents might be mad at themselves and embarrassed about trying to get you involved. They'll get over it. Even if you have to repeat yourself a few times and ask them to keep you out of the middle, they should eventually respond to your feelings.

Put Aside Your Guilt

Someone must have written a rule that goes like this: Every kid whose parents are getting divorced will feel guilty for one reason or another. To get through this tough time with some reasonable

WHERE SHOULD I GO?

You may feel inclined to disappear when tension builds around your house. Sometimes it's appropriate to go to your room or to go visit a friend for some relief. But when things quiet down again, it's important and mature for you to tell your parents how you feel. It's good for them to hear that you get angry and upset at the way they're treating each other. Your parents care about how you feel, and so it could be helpful for them to hear you express yourself right now.

It's not your fault if your parents are arguing a lot, and it's not your job to keep the peace. They're the grown-ups.

expectations of yourself, you'll have to get over the guilt . . . fast! Here are a few examples of other kids feeling guilty, and responses explaining why their parents' divorce was not their fault.

My parents were always arguing about the bills. I think they split up because of me, since all my extracurricular activities cost them a lot. — Sammi

If your parents are divorcing, the problems they are having are between the two of them. No child is the cause of his or her parents' divorce, even if the parents are quarreling over the child.

Your parents aren't getting a divorce because you spent too much money on clothes. Your shopping sprees had nothing to do with their relationship. Whatever the reason for their split, it's between them.

I think my parents are getting a divorce because my dad resents me for being born. Before I came along, my mom paid more attention to him. — Darius

It's not your fault that your parents don't fit well together anymore. Besides—whatever it is that broke them apart had nothing to do with how much they love you.

I can't understand why my parents got married in the first place. They don't have anything in common. They don't even seem to like each other. — Brianna

People change. Some marriages can weather the changes that people experience, but other times it's natural for people to grow apart. This is why most people get divorced.

My parents told me they're getting a divorce, and now it seems like all they do is fight about what to do with me. — Elias

If you feel as if your parents are fighting because of you, remember that their arguments are a symptom of deeper problems between the two of them. In other words, they would find something to argue about even if you were not around.

Keep reminding yourself that it's your parents' marriage that is ending; they're not going to stop being parents to you. If you have trouble remembering that the split has nothing to do with you, write down on a piece of paper over and over again that it's not your fault. Eventually, you'll get it!

CHAPTER THREE

CHANGES IN YOUR HOUSEHOLD

When parents divorce, the transition can be a complicated one. New routines take time to be established. This includes someone moving out of the household. It's tough to face the reality that soon one of your parents won't be living with you.

The Custody Decision

Custody establishes which parent a child or children will live with after a divorce. Some parents divide custody, which means that children divide their time between two households. This arrangement is known as joint custody. Other parents set up various systems in which children alternate homes from week to week.

How a family decides to handle custody depends on multiple factors that are unique to each family. The options are many. Sometimes custody starts out one way and ends up another. Usually when parents divorce, children end up spending more time with one parent than another. If your parents disagree about

In a custody battle, the responsibility of the family court judge is to determine what is in the best interest of the children. If you are asked to speak about your parents, do not feel that you are betraying one of them.

whom you will live with after the divorce, things can get complicated. This disagreement is sometimes referred to as a custody battle. Who retains custody is normally determined in family court. Family court is the sector of the judicial system that settles such matters.

You may be brought to court to testify in front of a judge about your own custodial issues. If you are, the questions might be difficult and awkward for you to answer openly since both parents might be seated in the courtroom. This is an extreme example of the tug-of-war that can happen between parents and their children during a divorce. Both parents will hire lawyers and present their sides of the story to a judge. Their lawyers will be very sympathetic with your awkward position, and they might even interview you in private. Rest assured, the family court has your best interest in mind when it makes its custody decision. You are absolutely its top priority.

Moving Out

Since it's been determined that your parents can't live together, someone's got to go. The easiest possible solution is that you

Chances are, one of your parents will move out of the family home. It will be a difficult adjustment without him or her living with you all the time. In some cases, everyone moves out. Either way, you'll have a new living situation.

will simply stay in the house or apartment where you are living now. However, you may have to move into a new place. If this is the case, the changes are coming so fast and furious that they might be overwhelming you.

The first thing that might change is your school, which will be an enormous adjustment. You might not be living as close to your old neighborhood friends anymore. Although it's crucial that you make every effort to adjust to your new school, it's also important to keep in touch with your old friends when possible. Let your parents know that doing so will make things a lot easier on you. If you're moving far away, you should make time to Skype or FaceTime or talk to them on the phone.

If it's the case that you are changing schools, be sure to introduce yourself to your new school counselor. He or she will be more than happy to show you around and tell you about the extra-curricular activities at your new school. Don't be afraid to tell him or her why you've switched schools—you're doing yourself a favor by increasing your support network.

A transition to a new neighborhood and school can be a little bit easier if you have siblings who are also going through the same thing. Support one another as you learn the ropes of your new surroundings.

When my mom said that she was moving out, I was shocked. I couldn't imagine life without my mom right there. What if she decided to move far away? Would she be around to see me graduate from high school? I didn't know if I had a choice to go with her or not. The whole thing was very scary at first. — Tom

WHEN A PARENT LASHES OUT AT YOU

Even though your parent legally has custody and may have even fought in court to keep you with him or her, raising a child and living alone is a major adjustment. In the midst of this adjustment, your parent may say hurtful things he or she doesn't mean. Keep in mind that your parent isn't perfect. Many of the things you are feeling right now, your parents are feeling, too. They may be the adults, but from time to time they'll act like children. They might be so sad and overwhelmed that they feel they don't know how to take care of you by themselves.

It takes a lot for a parent to care for a child by himself or herself. The strength to do this takes time to build, and in the meantime, you might be exposed to a couple of tantrums. Express how painful these tantrums are for you. If the tantrums persist after you've expressed how you feel, discuss this with an adult you trust, such as a grandparent or a school counselor.

Staying Put

If you continue to live where you were living before your parents' separation, you will still experience temporary inconveniences. The greatest challenge in this scenario is getting used to the absence of the parent who has moved away. This is a very disruptive and painful change—perhaps the most painful. Before your parents decided to get a divorce, they may have fought a lot, but they were probably both around a lot more. Now you'll have to call your newly absent mom or dad to tell him or her things that might seem small and insignificant. Remember that even the smallest thing you want to talk to your parents about is not insignificant right now. If you feel the need to talk to your absent parent, it's fine to pick up the phone and call.

Your Second Home

When one parent moves out, he or she will need somewhere to go. And you're going to need to visit him or her on weekends and maybe some days after school. This is called visitation, and it can be an annoying situation since you're forever packing up stuff and taking it from one place to another.

Your parent might have to move into a smaller home or one that's not as comfortable as your own. There might not be much furniture yet, and none of your stuff will be there. You might not like going there, but think about how difficult it was for your parent to move out. Most likely, he or she isn't comfortable yet either. Perhaps the two of you can shop for furniture or other decorations together to make the new place a little homier.

It's normal to look back on the bad times with both parents as better than life with the absence of a parent. But you'll breathe

When one parent picks you up from a vistation with the other parent, he or she might try to grill you about what you did and how the other parent is living. Tell your parent that makes you feel uncomfortable.

easier after your routine shifts and you grow used to the change. No matter how you look at it, there will be less tension in your house than there was.

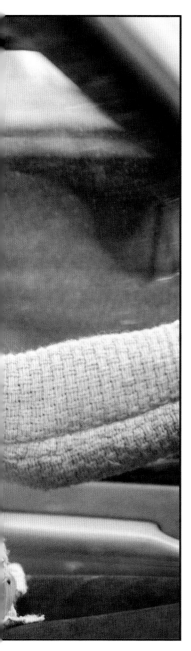

Over time you will discover that your relationships with your parents might change, even for the better. Your visits with your "absent" parent will probably be for more concentrated blocks of time than you're accustomed to with him or her. This might allow each of your parents to get to know and appreciate your relationship even more than he or she did before. Shaking things up will force everyone to get more creative about how to spend precious time together.

New Challenges You May Face

During this time, your parents might be feeling inadequate because they aren't used to providing for you on their own. Maybe your dad played baseball with you, but your mom simply doesn't know how to play. Or maybe it's a lot more complex than that: the parent who moved out is the one who used to listen to all the details of your day. This is a change that may make you feel terribly lonely.

In time, though, you'll adapt. Roles will change and so will your expectations. It might not be such a bad thing to shake things up a little bit. Your parents need to be forgiving of themselves during this major shift and realize that it takes time for new routines to fall into place. You will be a lot better off if you can be forgiving of some of their shortcomings right now.

If your parents separate with a lot of anger, you might find yourself caught in the middle. Unfortunately, when they are still angry, they don't always remember to keep you out of it. Your mom might feel insecure when you visit your dad, for instance, and worry that you prefer spending time with him. Here are some real-life experiences from kids of divorce that you might find yourself relating to.

When Tasha and Andre came home from a weekend away visiting their father, their mother was at home waiting for them, furious. "Where did your father take you?" "What did you do?" "Does he have a new girlfriend?" "Did he take you to a nice restaurant?" "What are those clothes he sent you home in?" "Does your father think he can buy your love?"

Sometimes when you go to visit your parent, you come home to an unreasonable line of questioning. This is a very upsetting thing for a parent to do to you, and it's not fair at all.

Even if your parents can't stand each other now, they are both still your parents, and it's not your fault they split up! So if you're coming home to this, tell your angry parent that you need to have the freedom to continue your relationship with your mother or father. Even if it makes him or her unhappy, your parent will grow to see that it's better for you in the long run to see both parents.

My father was so angry at my mother that he decided he couldn't talk to her on the phone anymore. Whenever he would drive me home from our visits, he would make me pass along information to her instead. "You tell your mother that I'm sick and tired of her calling me and yelling at me all the time." Of course, I wouldn't give my mom mean messages, but it got so annoying! — Daisy

Bearing the responsibility of delivering messages between one parent and another is unfair to you. Perhaps they're so angry that they don't want to talk to each other, or they can't do it without ending up in a screaming match. That's not your fault. If you begin to feel that your parents are being unreasonable and putting you in the middle, speak up. Even if they get mad at you, it's temporary. If you have to repeat yourself, you're still doing the right thing. Eventually, they'll hear you and begin communicating with each other.

CHAPTER FOUR

COPING WITH YOUR CHANGING LIFE

With all the new things happening as a result of your parents' divorce, it might seem that you're drifting increasingly farther away from life as you knew it. So how do you stay afloat? While there will be plenty of things that you have no control over, for sure, there also are plenty of things that are completely up to you.

The Power of Siblings

Do you have brothers and/or sisters? If so, they are going through the exact same thing you are. When you stop to think about it, siblings are pretty amazing. There is no other personal relationship in which the other person has shared your intimate childhood experiences, as your siblings did. Often this includes a lot of fighting—particularly in adolescence, when you are all trying to have your own space.

The time to stick together is during your parents' separation and divorce. There may be times when you feel like talking about it, but you don't want to discuss it with your friends. Another bonus about getting along well right now is that if you are having

Having a brother or sister can be a great benefit during a divorce. Your sibling will be going through the same pain and adjustment that you are. You can confide your feelings and offer your support to him or her.

to travel back and forth between your parents' homes, you will have an extra buffer of support when times feel lonely. It might take a while to make new friends in the new neighborhood.

My sister, Amy, and I always fought like cats and dogs, or so my mom always said. She is only one year older than me, and it seemed like we were always competing—at school, on the basketball court, and for boys. Normally, I'd rather spend time with my friends than with Amy, but when my parents told us they were separating, things changed. Suddenly Amy was the only person who really understood what I was feeling. When our mom moved us to another town, it really helped to have Amy there when I started a new school and had no friends. — Jeannette

WHERE TO FIND SUPPORT

Finding support might seem trickier for only children. But just because you don't have brothers and sisters doesn't mean that you have to feel isolated. You just need to be creative when discovering your support network. Ask yourself these important questions:

Who makes you feel good when you talk with him or her? Who do you tell your problems to? Do you feel close to your grandparents, or do any other relatives or friends of the family live nearby? If you go to church or synagogue, is there a member of the clergy whom you could speak with?

One way to feel some immediate relief from a painful and awkward home life is, simply, to step away from it sometimes. You aren't running away from your problems— you're just giving yourself a break. Answer the previous questions and then seek help from those who make you feel the most comfortable and loved.

Exercising Your Mind and Body

Exercise helps to fight depression. If you already participate in after-school sports, you know how much better you feel after running around for a couple of hours. Sports do more than strengthen your body; they strengthen your concentration and temporarily force you to focus only on the game. Extracurricular activities get you away from your house for a little while to hang out with other people your own age.

If you aren't interested in sports, take a good look at the other activities that are offered by your school, local boys and girls

During this stressful time, it will help to focus on something other than your problems. One great way to do this is to exercise. Not only is it healthy for the body, but it also helps clear the mind.

clubs, the YMCA . . . even your local library. All are jam-packed with interesting workshops that will broaden your interests, show you a good time, and introduce you to new people.

I didn't know how to deal with my parents' divorce, so I started acting out at school and at home. One day, my friend's dad took us for a hike to the top of a nearby mountain. Something about the fresh air and focusing on climbing the trails made me feel a lot better. I like to go back whenever I can. Looking out on the view from the top of the mountain makes my problems seem small. — Adam

Don't forget to have fun even during the pain of your parents' split. Having a strong community of friends will be a great source of support. And continuing your activities will give you something of your own to focus on.

Working your mind is as important as moving your body is. Be mindful of your creative urges right now. If you don't keep a journal, you may want to start one. Writing about your feelings, painting, or doing any other creative work could be an outlet that will keep you sane and occupied. Some of history's greatest artists created their best work when they were in painful situations.

Remember to Have Fun

Your parents have a lot on their minds right now. Chances are, entertaining you is not at the top of their list of priorities. Guess what? It needs to be on the top of your list.

Do yourself a huge favor and write down ten things that you enjoy doing that don't involve your parents' participation. Do you live close to a movie theater? Do you ride your bike or read a lot? When your parents are divorcing, it is incredibly important to continue doing whatever it is you enjoy doing. It's a strange by-product of divorce, but in the long run, you will be turning yourself into a more independent and creative person who knows yourself very well.

CHAPTER FIVE

MONEY MATTERS

There's a consequence of divorce that hasn't been discussed yet—and it's a big one. Maybe your family was well off financially. Or maybe your parents struggled to make ends meet. Or maybe you had no idea how much money your family had because no one ever discussed it. One thing you might notice, now that your parents are living in two different places, is that money becomes an issue.

Down to One Income

For every family that is separating, there is a unique financial restructuring that takes place. Suddenly, there isn't one, but two households to support. This means two rents or mortgages, two stocked refrigerators, and more.

For many families, this is a difficult adjustment. There simply isn't the money there used to be. This may mean you have to get a part-time job after school, and you might need to become conscious of your family's budget for the first time.

But whatever you do, don't drop out of school! If you really believe it might come to that, discuss the situation with your school guidance counselor. Your counselor will do everything he or she can to help you figure out a way to meet your obligations without allowing your education to suffer.

When my dad moved out, he was supposed to send my mom money to help us. She had always stayed home with us, and the job she got after they divorced didn't pay a lot. When Dad's checks were late, my mom would freak out. We couldn't go to the movies anymore, and we had to eat peanut butter sandwiches for dinner every night. I was worried that if this continued, we'd have to move into a shelter. — Howard

Divorce usually brings a change in finances. For a little while, at least, money might be tight. You may be asked to help out around the house while your parent takes on extra work, or perhaps you'll get a part-time job.

Under the Law

There are some forms of legal support that are in place to help your family make the financial adjustments that occur with a divorce. The following are a couple of terms that you might be hearing right now. Child support is a monthly payment made by the parent who does not live with the child. This is a legal arrangement that is designed to help the supporting parent meet the children's needs. The law bases the amount on three factors: 1) the parents' combined income, 2) the prior lifestyle of the family, and 3) the children's needs.

IDEAS FOR SAVING MONEY

If money was never an issue when your parents were together, you might find tightening your belt now more difficult. But there are plenty of ways to save money. First, work with a parent to develop a budget. Then find creative ways to stick to it, such as:

- Shop for clothes and books at your neighborhood thrift stores.
- Help your parent collect coupons (you can double the worth of these at many grocery stores).
- Find out where you can use a student ID for reduced admission to cultural events (many museums let students in for free).
- Rediscover your library for free and fun workshops, movie rentals, and even reduced-fee tutoring.

The amount of this payment differs greatly from family to family. Some parents' payments are higher if there are education or medical needs to be met.

Sadly, some households have difficulty collecting these payments. Paying child support is a serious obligation that parents have after a divorce. Family courts are in place to help parents fight for their rights if the need for legal help arises.

Fortunately, laws are getting tougher. Garnishing wages (automatically deducting money from a parent's paycheck in the same way that taxes are automatically taken out) is one way family courts obtain these payments. A similar arrangement to child support is spousal support. This is a legal payment arrangement designed by our legal system to assure that a former spouse can maintain, as well as possible, his or her previous lifestyle and meet his or her needs.

Get to Work!

Finding a part-time job is a terrific way to help your household out financially. Before you do this, have a talk with your custodial parent about what contributions he or she thinks would be fair so that you won't be surprised after you bring home your first paycheck.

Have some ideas of your own to contribute to this conversation. For example, maybe you like picking out your own clothes when you go shopping. Picking up the tab for new clothes you might need is a way for you to help out and to become more independent. Another way you can pitch in is with your school expenses: books, uniforms, and other fees that come up throughout the academic year. Even taking a bite out of your allowance could help your parent to manage your newly reduced household budget better.

Think about your location, your access to public transportation, and your homework load before you consider where to look for a job. All of these elements need to be factored into your choice. Finally, think about what you enjoy doing. Do you like hanging out at the mall with your friends after school? Why not try approaching some of your favorite stores to see if they could use your help for a few hours a week? If you simply have too much homework to consider working during the year, get a jump on researching summer jobs, such as camp counselor.

Here are some other places you could look: your local library, restaurants and coffee shops in your neighborhood, neighbors who may need babysitters or landscapers, hardware stores, or bookstores. Use your imagination!

Aside from earning you some extra pocket money, working part-time has lots of other benefits. Having a job looks great on your résumé when you are applying to colleges, and many colleges would favor someone who can get a written recommendation from a boss. It's one way to prove to people how

Working as a stocker or cashier at a grocery store is just one example of a part-time job that you might consider if you would like to help your family financially. You will juggle this responsibility with your homework.

responsible you are. Your part-time job could introduce you to new friends, teach you many skills, get you out of the house during a difficult time, and just be a lot of fun.

Help your parent by taking on more responsibility around the house. Teens are able to do chores like laundry, cleaning, preparing or starting dinner, and watching younger siblings.

Help Out Around the House

If the parent you live with also works, don't underestimate the power of housework as a tool to help keep the household running smoothly. During this stressful adjustment, helping out around the house will make everyone a lot happier.

Perhaps you get home after school earlier than your working parent does. You can use some of this time to straighten up the house and even get a head start on dinner. Babysitting younger siblings and mowing the lawn are other ways you could help out and even save your parent some money. Everybody's energy is precious right now, and a clean house might be exactly what your family needs.

If you have siblings who are old enough to help you out, take charge and parcel out chores in a way that is fair. Alternate so that you don't get too bored being responsible for the same things; for example, one of you can vacuum while the other washes the dishes.

CHAPTER SIX

WHEN YOUR PARENTS REMARRY

When your parents divorce, you have to adjust to a whole new way of life. Eventually this new life will seem normal. But there might be another change on the horizon. Once the dust settles after a divorce, your parents may start dating other people. Many will remarry. When that happens, they create what is called a binuclear family. This means that where there was once one family and one household, there are now two.

Dealing with an Awkward Transition

As with so many other aspects of divorce, the results of this transition vary from family to family. Some parents may gain stepchildren if they marry someone who already has children. For their own children, this is very difficult. Suddenly they may feel jealous and angry about their growing family.

And this transition can be just as difficult for those kids entering an already-existing family. They may feel resentful and

Blended families, even the Kardashians and Jenners, can take some time to get used to each other. It is awkward to suddenly live with people you don't know very well.

behave badly. It can feel awkward to move in with people you don't know very well.

After a few years of living with just my mom and brothers, my mom got married again, to the father of one of my classmates. I was happy for Mom, but it was really strange having to live with this boy I knew from school. Not to mention his dad, who felt like a stranger even though Mom had brought him around a little. — Dorie

Just remember that for this time, families are reorganizing themselves. Once years go by and your parents are with other people, it may be strange for you to visualize how life was before the divorce. For a lot of parents who get divorced and remarry, marriage feels more natural and happier for them the second time around.

After the dust settles, you might be surprised. While it can be difficult following two sets of household rules, some kids actually enjoy the change of pace of going back and forth between one place and another. It gives them a chance to enjoy two different lifestyles.

A Blended Family

If you have siblings already, you know how intense these relationships can be. You either get along really well, or you fight like cats and dogs. Maybe you fall somewhere in between. Whatever your relationship is to them, one thing is for sure: you see them a lot.

Inheriting new brothers and sisters, called stepsiblings, when a parent remarries is a bizarre situation. If you already have

While ultimately you will appreciate having a half sibling, you may feel left out initially if your parent has a child with his or her new spouse. Look at the experience as something you and your parent can share.

siblings, the addition of stepsiblings can upset the dynamic you've established over your lives together. If you have grown up as an only child, the transition can be even more jarring. Suddenly having to share your home and parent with someone else's kids can be difficult to deal with.

Even more confusing than inherited siblings are the children that your parent might have with his or her new spouse, your half sibling. If you don't live with the "new" family during the week, you may have to spend weekends with them. It can be weird to see your parent cooing over a new baby. After all, you came first, and it's hard to believe that there is enough attention to go around.

My dad and his new wife had a baby three years ago. At first, all they talked about was the baby, and they forgot all about me. Eventually, my dad started spending more time with me, and my stepmom let me feed and hold the baby. Now my little brother is waiting for me when I come home

FAMOUS BLENDED FAMILIES

With so many divorces and remarriages among celebrities, there are plenty of blended families in the spotlight. While it may seem that they have merged seamlessly, the truth is probably that, like in most blended families, there was an awkward transition period in adjusting to the situation. Some famous blended families are:

- **The Kardashians.** Kris Kardashian already had four children when she married Caitlyn Jenner (known as Bruce prior to her transition), who had children of her own from previous marriages.
- **The Brady Bunch.** This fictional family blended three daughters from one marriage with three sons from another.
- **The Smiths.** When Jaden and Willow Smith were born, they joined Trey Smith, Will's son from a previous marriage and Jada's stepson.
- **The Jolie-Pitts.** Angelina Jolie had already adopted her son Maddox when she met her now-husband Brad Pitt. Pitt adopted Maddox, who was soon joined by a brood of brothers and sisters.

from school every day. I can't wait to teach him how to play soccer in a few years. — Angel

At first, it's true that there might not be enough attention for you. Your parents are adjusting to a new life, and it is probably pretty hard for them to try to juggle everything and everyone. Just as you are having a tough time with the changes, your stepparents' children are probably having an equally tough time. There is sure to be some tension somewhere, and to get through all this, it's helpful to remember a couple of things.

You did come first, and your parents love the special relationship that they have with you and you alone. No one can replace the position you have in their hearts. You might be surprised and find yourself liking things about your stepsiblings.

Try to be open to new relationships—and give yourself a break! It's natural to feel jealous, confused, and upset about all of this. After some time passes, you will have a different perspective on what these new fixtures in your life can mean to you. Besides, it may be nice to see your parent happy again.

Adapting to Your New Stepparent

Traveling from place to place before your parent remarried was hard enough. Now dealing with this new kind of parent in your life may feel awkward. One difficult thing about stepparents is certain to crop up: suddenly you have to adhere to a new set of rules— theirs. Every parent has a unique philosophy about how to raise his or her children, and that includes your new stepparents. If they express their views about your behavior or about anything else, you may feel like they're overstepping their

Stepmothers get a bad rap because of some fairy tales, like Cinderella. But most stepparents are not evil and instead want the best for you. Give them a chance and try to get to know them.

boundaries. If this is the case, the best thing you can do is to keep the lines of communication open between you and your birth parent. By doing this, you prove that you are willing to give your stepparent a chance, but you need to talk about how he or she interacts with you.

Help keep your parents close to you instead of pushing them away. Your parents are prepared for some conflict, hurt, and confusion in their children when they remarry. If you talk openly with them, you'll also be giving them the opportunity to discuss their feelings with you.

When One Parent Stays Single

If you live with a parent who hasn't remarried while the other one has, you're bound to feel some loyalty toward your single parent. Your single parent is only human, and your other parent's remarriage will be difficult to adjust to, even if that period of adjustment is only temporary. If you felt a tug-of-war scenario when you were going back and forth before the remarriage, be prepared for the guilt to increase.

One natural reaction that kids have after going home to their single parent is to bad-mouth their stepparent to their single parent so the single parent will feel better. You might be coming home to a whole new third-degree line of questioning about your mother or father's "new lifestyle." Sometimes it seems easier to go along with your upset parent's feelings, but at what cost? The longer this goes on, the worse you will feel. Your parent needs to be the grown-up and accept

Don't feel guilty if you actually like your new stepparent. He or she is not replacing your father or mother. Think of him or her as an additional supportive person in your life.

that you are building a relationship with a new stepparent. If the third-degree continues to await you every time you come home, stand your ground and tell your parent how lousy it makes you feel. Eventually, your mom or dad will hear you, and you won't have to feel bad when you come home anymore.

When I went to visit my mom and her new husband, Frank, this weekend, we actually had a pretty good time. They took me to the movies, and we did some shopping. But when I came home to my dad, I felt totally guilty that Frank had taken me to a ballgame because my dad has been working two jobs and doesn't have much time to do fun things. So I didn't tell him about the game, and I told him that I couldn't stand Frank. Now I feel guilty for lying, and I worry that my dad will be sad if I tell him I actually kind of like Frank. — Ayden

When divorce happens, there will be both ups and downs for a long, long time. But trust in the power of time, and tap into the strength you have inside yourself, and you'll get through it. Nothing can erase the bond you have with your family members. And as all of your lives change, you can make sure that these bonds always stay strong.

GLOSSARY

ALIMONY Another term for spousal support. Money paid by one person to his or her spouse for a period of time after a divorce.

BINUCLEAR FAMILY A term that describes the process of both parents remarrying: where there was once one family and one household, there are now two.

BLENDED FAMILY A family made up of two parents, their children from previous relationships, and children that result from their own union.

CHILD SUPPORT A monthly payment made by the parent who does not live with the child. This is a legal arrangement that is designed to help the supporting parent meet his or her children's needs.

CUSTODIAL PARENT The parent awarded custody of the children, with whom they live and who cares for them.

CUSTODY The legal decision that establishes with which parent a child or children will live after a divorce.

DIVORCE The legal ending of a marriage.

FAMILY COURT A legal system that is set up to fairly process all legal matters having to do with divorce, such as child support payments, custody, and other legal issues that arise in families.

GARNISHED WAGE Money automatically deducted from a parent's paycheck to go toward child support.

INCONVENIENCE Trouble or difficulty.

JOINT CUSTODY Divided custody in which the children divide their time between both parents.

RECONCILE To make up, or repair relations.

SIBLING A brother or sister.

SPOUSAL SUPPORT Another term for alimony. Similar to child support, spousal support is a legal payment arrangement designed to assure that a former spouse can maintain, as well as possible, his or her previous lifestyle.

STEPPARENT A stepmother or stepfather; a person who marries a child's parent.

TENSION Stress or emotional strain.

VISITATION A formally arranged meeting between the children and their noncustodial parent. This can be a brief visit or an extended stay.

FOR MORE INFORMATION

Al-Anon Family Group Headquarters, Inc.
1600 Corporate Landing Parkway
Virginia Beach, VA 23454
(757) 563-1600
Website: http://www.al-anon.org
Th Al-Anon site can link you to local Al-Anon meetings—a great
place to go for help if you live with an alcoholic parent or
stepparent.

American Association for Marriage and Family Therapy
112 South Alfred Street
Alexandria, VA 22314-3061
(703) 838-9808
Website: http://www.aamft.org
This organization offers support and suggestions for seeking
family therapy to cope with divorce and blended families.

Childhelp USA Hotline
(800) 422-4453
This hotline is available in English and Spanish for young people
in crisis.

Children's Rights Council
1296 Cronson Blvd.
Suite 3086
Crofton, MD 21114
(301) 459-1220
Website: http://www.crckids.org
The Children's Rights Council is dedicated to helping divorced,
separated, and never-married parents remain actively and

responsibly involved in their children's lives. Parents can join local groups to help them deal with their situation.

Erika's Lighthouse
897 1/2 Green Bay Road
Winnetka, IL 60093
(847) 386-6481
Website: http://www.erikaslighthouse.org
This organization educates and empower teens to take charge
of their mental health.

Stepfamily Foundation
310 West 85th Street
Suite 1B
New York, NY 10024
(212) 877-3244
Website: http://www.stepfamily.org
This nonprofit organization provides counseling for the step-
family/blended family, divorce counseling, remarriage
counseling, and stepfamily certification seminars.

Websites

Because of the changing nature of Internet links, Rosen Publishing has developed an online list of websites related to the subject of this book. This site is updated regularly. Please use this link to access this list:
http://www.rosenlinks.com/DIV/feel

FOR FURTHER READING

Baker, Amy J. L., and Katherine Andre. *Getting Through My Parents' Divorce*. Oakland, CA: Instant Help Books, 2015.

Bergin, Rory M., and Jared Meyer. *Frequently Asked Questions About Divorce*. New York, NY: Rosen Publishing, 2012.

Bryfonski, Dedria. *Child Custody*. Farmington Hills, MI: Greenhaven Press, 2011.

Espejo, Roman. *Custody and Divorce*. Detroit, MI: Greenhaven Press, 2013.

Gay, Kathlyn. *Divorce: The Ultimate Teen Guide*. Lanham, MD: Rowman & Littlefield, 2014.

Iorizzo, Carrie. *Divorce and Blended Families*. St. Catharines, Ontario: Crabtree Publishing Company, 2013.

Kavanaugh, Dorothy. *Hassled Girl?: Girls Dealing with Feelings*. Berkeley Heights, NJ: Enslow Publishers, 2014.

McLaughlin, Jerry, and Katherine E. Krohn. *Dealing with Your Parents' Divorce*. New York, NY: Rosen Publishing, 2016.

Peterman, Rosie L., Jared Meyer, and Charlie Quill. *Divorce and Stepfamilies*. New York, NY: Rosen Publishing, 2013.

Stewart, Sheila, and Rae Simons. *I Live in Two Homes: Adjusting to Divorce and Remarriage*. Broomall, PA: Mason Crest Publishers, 2011.

INDEX

legal, 40
for only children, 34
siblings as, 26, 32–33
spousal, 41

T

tension at home, 7, 16, 18, 28,
    51

U

uncertainty, 12

V

visitation, 27

About the Authors

Viola Jones teaches middle school and writes books for young adults. She lives in the Hudson River valley with her husband and daughters.

Rachel Aydt has worked in magazines and book publishing in New York City. She has published several magazine articles and two books of poetry.

Photo Credits

Cover Ampyang/Shutterstock.com; back cover, pp. 4-5 © iStockphoto.com/jsmith; p. 5 Jamie Grill/Getty Images; pp. 8-9 threerocksimages/Shutterstock.com; p. 10 Gary S Chapman/Getty Images; p. 12 Altrendo/Getty Images; p. 15 Andrew Olney/Stockbyte/Getty Images; p. 17 Monkey Business Images/Shutterstock; p. 19 Tetra Images/Getty Images; pp. 22-23 Image Source/Getty Images; pp. 24-25 David Seed Photography/Photographer's Choice/Getty Images; pp. 28-29 Maskot/Getty Images; p. 33 Volt Collection/Shutterstock.com; p. 35 Catalin Petolea/Shutterstock.com; p. 36 oliveromg/Shutterstock.com; pp. 39, 44 JGI/Jamie Grill/Blend Images/Getty Images; pp. 42-43 moodboard/Cultura/Getty Images; p. 47 Donaldson Collection/Michael Ochs Archives/Getty Images; p. 49 Floresco Productions/Cultura/Getty Images; pp. 52-53 © Photos 12/Alamy Stock Photo; p. 54 Linda Yolanda/E+/Getty Images; interior pages textured background chungking/Shutterstock.com

Designer: Nicole Russo; Editor: Christine Poolos; Photo Researcher: Karen Huang